# TASMANIA

# Tasmania

JOE SHEMESH • MIKE BINGHAM

NEW HOLLAND

First published in Australia in 1998 by
New Holland Publishers (Australia) Pty Ltd
Sydney • Auckland • London • Cape Town

14 Aquatic Drive Frenchs Forest NSW 2086 Australia
1A, 278 Lake Road Northcote Auckland New Zealand
24 Nutford Place London W1H6DQ United Kingdom
80 McKenzie Street Cape Town 8001 South Africa

National Library of Australia
Cataloguing-in-Publication data:

Bingham, Mike, 1941- .
  Tasmania.
Includes index.
ISBN 1 86436 338 X.
1. Tasmania - Pictorial works. I. Shemesh, Joe. II. Title.
919.4600222

Publishing General Manager: Jane Hazell
Publisher: Averill Chase
All photographs by Joe Shemesh with the exception of
pages 6, 11, 104 (right and below) by Craig Johnson AND??
Editors: Julie Nekich, Emma Wise and Anouska Good
Designer: Mandy McKay
Reproduction by Unifoto (Pty) Ltd, Cape Town
Printed and bound in Singapore by Tien Wah Press (Pty) Ltd

Captions for photographs on previous pages:
HALF-TITLE PAGE: Thousands of plane passengers from Strahan
on the West Coast wander through the rainforest at Sir John Falls.
TITLE PAGE: The superb beach at Boat Harbour, near Wynyard
on the North-West Coast, is backed by some of the island's
richest farmlands. The milk from the dairy herds in the region
is used to make high quality cheeses which are exported
nationally and internationally.
THIS PAGE: The Marble Cliffs, and the superb reflections they
create on the Gordon River, close to the confluence of the
Franklin River.

# CONTENTS

# FOREWORD

*by Margaret Scott*

ABOVE: *A crop of peas in flower at Sassafras near Devonport on the North-West Coast.*
LEFT: *Federation Peak, in the South-West National Park, rises from one of the most remote and rugged regions in Australia — scenic overflights offer spectacular views of the area.*

When I first arrived in Tasmania 1960, Hobart seemed a dull and dusty little town, full of clanking trams. There were no restaurants other than a solitary Chinese establishment and a couple of cavernous hotels patronised by the squattocracy. The sea and bush, pressing around the city, struck me not as beautiful but as menacing. Nature there was too huge and too untamed. I had a nasty feeling that, if it chose, it could flatten Hobart's fragile weatherboard suburbs in the twinkling of an eye.

Seven years later, when southern Tasmania was devastated by the worst bushfires in living memory, these forebodings proved well founded, but by then my attitude to the island state had altered. I no longer hated it for not being England and had begun to admire the scenery. Soon I would become so obsessed with the place that I could never think of living anywhere else. And so, after thirty odd years, I'm still here in the home I have come to love with an absolute passion.

Tasmania has, of course, changed a great deal since 1960. Increasing awareness of the need to conserve historic sites and structures as well as the natural environment has gone hand in hand with development of the state's tourist industry. In Hobart's Salamanca Place, for instance, the old warehouses have been carefully restored and new, elegantly presented attractions introduced. Restaurants of every conceivable kind now spread from this central area across the city. On the West Coast Strahan has changed from a fishing village and mining port to an ecotourism centre, gateway to an expanse of World Heritage wilderness.

Joe Shemesh and Mike Bingham have covered a lot of ground, providing pen-portraits and stunning visual images of these and many other Tasmanian places. Sections like The East and Tasmania's Islands indicate how many secrets Tasmania holds, how much richness lies concealed. Yet, I have my own experiences of the particular areas mentioned. When you travel to Port Arthur you may see nothing of what is hidden away on either side of the main tourist route: the magnificent arc of white sand at Slopen Main, the convict coal mines at Salt Water River. When you visit Flinders Island it may be nobody will tell you about flying over the strait between Flinders and Cape Barren Island in one of the islander's planes to see the wreck of the *Farsund*. Unless you ask around you might never hear how the old ship was trapped in the treacherous 'Potboil' over 70 years ago.

Tasmania is a treasure-trove of stories — some tragic, some thrilling, some comic, like the tale of the Maria Island entrepreneur who conned his backers by tying bunches of grapes to his barren vines. Perhaps this is why the state has produced so many remarkable writers, ranging from Christopher Koch to Richard Flanagan, and why so many others, along with artists of all kinds, are drawn to settle here. You can live such a vibrant life in Tasmania, creating new images and new stories from the heart-stopping sights and entrancing tales which are there all around you, waiting to be discovered.

Margaret Scott

# Introduction

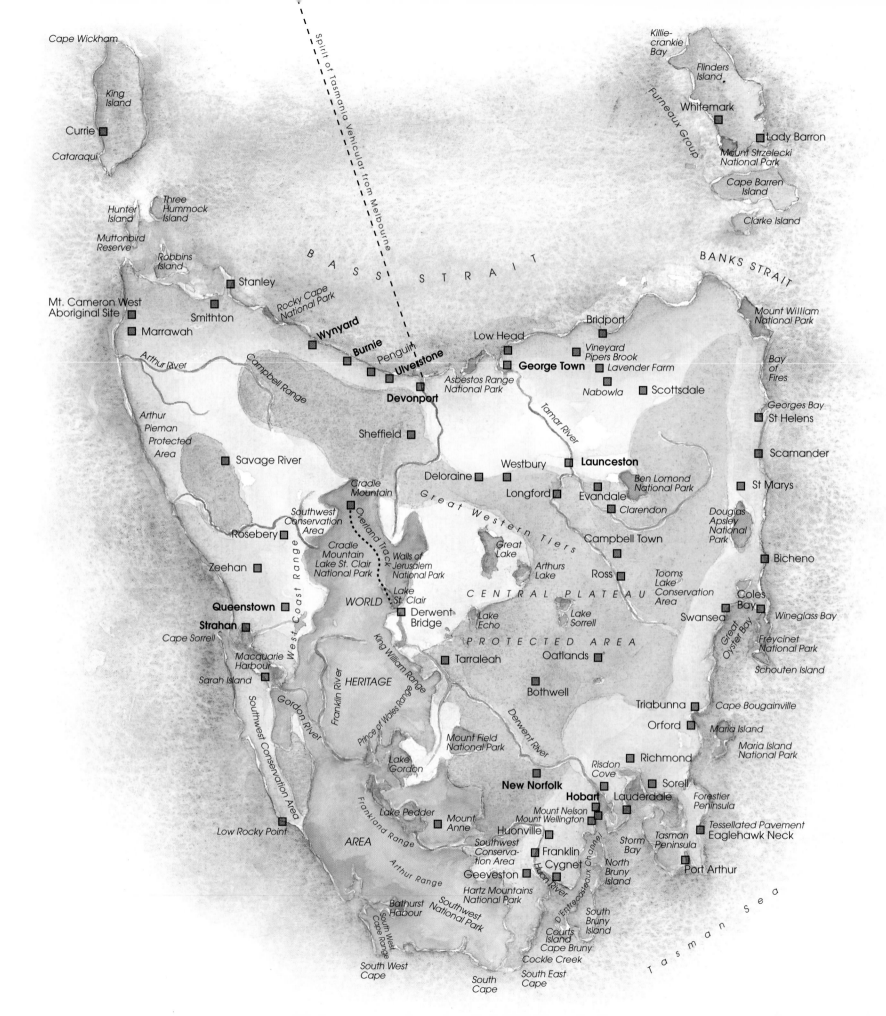

# INTRODUCTION

*A world apart*

Tasmania, Australia's friendly island state, seems a world away from the vast continent to its north. Delightfully diverse, the island's compact 67 840 square kilometres provide visitors and locals easy access to a richness of experience and terrain. From mountain wildernesses with deep glacial lakes and ancient forests to wild, storm-battered coasts, impossibly pristine beaches and some of the nation's richest farmlands and most important convict ruins, Tasmania offers a breadth of experience that is unequalled in Australia.

With an estimated population of only 500 000, Tasmania's air is free of pollution, the pace of life is slower, communities are smaller, and people have time to stop and chat — in country areas, it's still common practice while driving to acknowledge oncoming motorists with a wave of the hand or a nod. The people are known especially for their open and friendly acceptance of visitors; and while visitor information centres dot the island, most locals are happy to help with directions and recommendations.

Tasmania's maritime climate (no place in Tasmania lies more than 115 kilometres from the sea) is also friendly. While it is rarely too hot or too cold, there are significant climatic variations between regions. The wilder mountainous areas often experience sudden changes in weather, so cold-weather gear should always be taken when walking. Autumn is generally the most stable and pleasant of the seasons, but the East Coast is mild year-round, with cloudless winter skies and temperatures often several degrees above the West Coast and inland regions. Surprisingly, Hobart, which receives only 580 millimetres of rain a year, is Australia's second driest capital after Adelaide, while areas on the West Coast can record 2500 millimetres a year.

ABOVE: *Snow may fall at any time on the Cradle Mountain-Lake St Clair Overland Track.*
PREVIOUS PAGES: *The beach at Cox Bight, on the South Coast walk from Cockle Creek to Bathurst Harbour, provides a landing strip for light planes — weather and tides permitting.*

Tasmania has recognised the importance of it's ecological heritage by leading the way in Australia in preserving the natural environment. Twenty per cent of the island has been proclaimed World Heritage area, with a further 10 national parks outside its boundaries — in all, a quarter of Tasmania is a national park or reserve. Tasmania boasts a strong conservation movement — four Greens sit in the 35-member state Legislative Assembly — which has been campaigning for even greater protection.

Today the island, which is 200 kilometres south of Victoria across Bass Strait and was first seen by Europeans in 1642, has come to claim a place in the modern world where an apparently idyllic lifestyle seems to coexist with the natural environment better than anywhere else on earth. It has been an extraordinary transition from an isolated island inhabited by Aboriginal people through convict colony and industrial revolution to the Tasmania of today which, increasingly, embraces tourism and the environment as essential for creating jobs and maintaining lifestyle.

The story of European settlement begins more than 350 years ago with a Dutch voyage of exploration searching for information about the land far to the south of the Dutch East Indies

ABOVE: *Yachts at rest at Constitution Dock — the busy home of Hobart's fishing fleet.*

BELOW: *This simple monument at Risdon Cove records the original 1803 settlement.*

OPPOSITE TOP: *Afternoon light on the bare hills of Queenstown on the West Coast.*

OPPOSITE BELOW: *Tourists visit the haunting ruins of the Port Arthur Historic Site.*

(Indonesia). Abel Janszoon Tasman had sailed from Batavia (Jakarta) in August 1642 on a voyage ordered by the governor, Anthony van Diemen. He went by way of Mauritius in two small ships, the *Heemskirk* and the *Zeehan*, and then sailed east, making the first sighting of the West Coast of Tasmania on 24 November 1642, near the two mountains which now bear the names of his ships.

He named his discovery Anthony van Diemensland in honour of the governor and sailed south around the coastline to Marion Bay (near present-day Dunalley) where some of his men landed on 2 December. There is no record of Tasman himself setting foot on the island and no contact was made with the Tasmanian Aboriginal people, although smoke was seen in the distance and presumed to indicate human habitation. The men also noted notches cut in the trunks of trees, and judged that these were made by natives to enable them to climb to birds' nests. And, in what was the first reference

ever made to the Tasmanian tiger, animal prints 'not unlike the paws of a tiger' were seen.

The following day, Tasman sent another landing party to plant a flag and claim the land for the company. The weather was too rough for a boat to reach the beach so the ship's carpenter was ordered to take the flag and swim ashore. One of Tasman's officers recorded in his diary: 'This work having been duly executed, we pulled back to the ships, leaving the above-mentioned [flag] as a memorial for those who shall come after us, and for the natives of this country who did not show themselves, though we suspect some of them were at no great distance and closely watching our proceedings'. Two days later, on 5 December 1642, the expedition continued on to New Zealand, and it would be another 130 years before the arrival of the next European, French explorer Marc-Joséph Marion Du Fresne.

He called in search of fresh water and timber with which to repair one of his ships and anchored in Frederick Henry Bay on 6 March 1772, close to where Tasman's ships had also anchored. A party of about 30 Aboriginal people watched from the beach and the following day Du Fresne and his men landed in two boats. The initial contact between them was friendly and an exchange of gifts took place, but the approach of a third longboat alarmed the Aboriginal people and began the tragedy that culminated a century later with the death of Truganini, the last full-blood Tasmanian Aborigine.

As one of Du Fresne's officers reported: 'The savages showered us with a hail of hatchets and stones, one of which hit Du Fresne on the shoulder ... We fired a few shots and they quickly took flight, uttering some horrible screams'. A second attempt by the French to land soon after resulted in another clash and this time several of the 'Van Diemenlanders' were wounded and at least one killed.

After visiting Maria Island on the East Coast, Du Fresne, like Tasman before him, headed for New Zealand, only to be killed in a clash with the local inhabitants, the Maoris.

In 1803, the British became the first Europeans to settle in Tasmania, mainly to thwart any French aspirations to claim the island. Lieutenant John Bowen was sent from New South Wales with a party of soldiers and convicts and landed at Risdon Cove, upstream from present-day Hobart. Like Du Fresne before him, there was an armed clash with the Aboriginal people, followed by several deaths.

In February the following year, David Collins set out from Sydney to establish a settlement in Port Phillip Bay and, finding the landing area unsuitable, headed south to Hobart. Within weeks he had transferred the Risdon group to Sullivans Cove, drawn by the area's freshwater supply from the rivulet running down from Mount Wellington.

For the next half century, Tasmania would become the British Empire's most notorious prison. More than 70 000 convicts were landed before transportation ceased in 1857; Macquarie Harbour and Port Arthur came to be known as 'hell on earth'. Convicts felled Huon pine and worked coal mines in deplorable conditions, chain gangs formed the roads and constructed the bridges and substantial public buildings and, in the early days, public executions were a common sight in central Hobart.

Port Arthur is today the nation's most important convict site. Established in 1830 to exploit rich timber resources on the Tasman Peninsula, it gradually grew into a substantial settlement. Its isolation — with virtually all escape attempts blocked by the infamous 'dog line' across the narrow isthmus at Eaglehawk Neck — made it an ideal prison. It closed in 1877 and, ironically, created the beginnings of the Tasmanian tourist industry as some of the old convicts eked out a living guiding people around the settlement after its closure. Like tour guides everywhere, the ex-convicts included shock-horror anecdotes about the area, in this case from their own experiences.

Today, Tasmania's most valuable industry is mining, mostly concentrated on the West Coast. Extraction of copper, gold, iron ore, tin, lead,

ABOVE: *Hopfields at Bushy Park in the Derwent Valley near New Norfolk form the heart of Australia's hopgrowing industry. In the 1860s more than 2600 people were employed as pickers.*

BELOW: *Southern Tasmania's Dutch community turns out in force each October to celebrate the tulip festival in the Royal Tasmanian Botanic Gardens.*

The state leads the nation in aquaculture — the Atlantic salmon harvest alone now exceeds 8000 tonnes a year with fish growing from 80 grams to four kilograms in 12 to 15 months, the fastest growing rate in the world thanks to the ideal conditions. Tasmania also farms sea-run trout, oysters, scallops and mussels — and lands the best of the scalefish from the edge of the continental shelf, along with crayfish, abalone, squid, octopus, and king crabs; lobster (crayfish) and abalone remain major exports.

In recent years, however, Tasmanians, driven by a decline in heavy industry and a lack of investment, the nation's highest unemployment rate, and a continuing drain of young people to other states, are beginning to turn to tourism as a key element of their future.

'Bed and Breakfast' flourishes in convict-built cottages, small farms and elegant Georgian town-houses. Colonial villages such as Richmond, Ross and Stanley are little changed from the middle of last century, and Hobart's commercial heart, alone of the Australian state capitals, retains a large part of its sandstone streetscapes, and a fishing fleet and yachts at the bottom of its central business district.

As seductive as the echoes of the colonial era are, it is the environment which gives the island its greatest appeal, and a powerful and committed conservation movement has struggled hard to protect this asset. While Lake Pedder was flooded in 1972 despite a campaign by conservationists, 10 years later the identity of the island as one of the last great wilderness areas on earth began in earnest.

National and international attention focused on the 1982 struggle by protesters to stop the damming of one of Tasmania's last wild rivers, the lower Gordon. The issue sharply divided the community, particularly at Strahan which was the starting point for the protests. In the aftermath, Strahran has seen millions of dollars of development and has emerged as Tasmania's wilderness 'capital'.

Towns throughout Tasmania now offer a wide variety of activity-based holidays, from

zinc and coal has underpinned the general economy for over 120 years and now generates more than $1.2 billion per year in total sales.

Agriculture is also important as farmers produce about $570 million in turnover each year. Vegetable growing and dairying are the biggest contributors, and the single most valuable crop is potatoes (bringing in $61 million). Of course, the 'Apple Isle' also produces 52 000 tonnes of apples — three quarters of them in the Huon Valley south of Hobart.

The agricultural scene is diversifying rapidly as the island seeks to take advantage of improved air and shipping links to international markets such as Asia. Grapes, opium poppies for the pharmaceutical industry, walnuts, olives, saffron, essential oils, flowers, and Asian vegetables are among the relative newcomers.

Fishing, a traditional industry of the economy since earliest colonial times, brings in close to $200 million a year, with aquaculture becoming increasingly important as natural fish and shell-fish stocks have been reduced by overfishing.

white-water rafting, bushwalking, trout fishing, diving and trail-riding, trading on the state's eco-friendly image, to gourmet tours offering the best of Tasmania's produce. In Hobart itself, a strong tradition of walking on Mount Wellington, dates back to late last century. The local walking club has a membership of around 2000 and older members recall the days when a series of huts — from the rough to the elegant (one even had a piano) — dotted the mountain, providing bases for weekend getaways.

There are four natural gateways to any modern exploration of the island — Hobart, Launceston, Devonport and Strahan — and the temptation for first-time visitors is to try to see them all, and everything in between, in a week. It's possible to make the run around the state in that time, but it would mean sacrificing a true taste of the lifestyle. In any case, Tasmanian roads are generally quite narrow and winding, more suited to a leisurely exploration of the island.

Hobart, at the base of Mount Wellington, is Tasmania's oldest city, and provides easy access to most of the south. Today, the city is most famous for hosting the finish of the Sydney–Hobart Yacht Race. The race generally attracts around 100 entries, including several from outside Australia, and is one of the world's bluewater classics. It is traditional for thousands of spectators to be on hand to greet the winners — even if they arrive in the middle of the night.

The headquarters of the Australian Antarctic Division, Hobart is also establishing itself as an important centre for Antarctic research. In addition, it is home port of the division's supply ship Aurora Australis, and a providoring point for other nation's research ships.

Launceston, only a year younger than Hobart and a fierce rival of the capital, is the centre of the north, with the Tamar Valley and Pipers River vineyards, the city itself, and historic townships such as Longford, Evandale and Deloraine topping its list of attractions.

Devonport, home of the Bass Strait vehicular ferry, *Spirit of Tasmania*, is within 90 minutes of Cradle Mountain and is the main entry point to

LEFT: *A reflective moment on the often wild and always beautiful Gordon River on Tasmania's rugged West Coast.*

BELOW: *Richmond, near Hobart, is a classic colonial village tracing its beginnings back to the 1820s.*

BOTTOM: *The clear waters of Boat Harbour beach on the North-West Coast offer good swimming, diving and fishing.*

TOP: *Salamanca Place in Hobart with the colourful Saturday open-air market in full swing. The sandstone warehouses, built at the height of the whaling industry in the 1840s, are now home to artists, galleries, offices, cafes and restaurants.*

the North-West coast. It also has daily airlinks to Melbourne, as does Wynyard further along the coast. Strahan, on the West Coast, once a sleepy fishing village, is today the gateway to the spectacular south-west wilderness.

Tasmania — so much diversity and so easy to explore. The wilderness is never more than an hour away and is often much closer. A quaint Georgian village, with vineyards and opium poppy farms on its outskirts, is only an hour from a mountaintop view across some of the most rugged and isolated wilderness on earth. You can breakfast in Hobart, and cruise on the Gordon River on the West Coast in the afternoon. Or board a sailing ship at the bottom of a Hobart street to sail the Derwent for an hour or two before lunching at a waterfront restaurant.

The Cataract Gorge, with its picnic grounds, chairlift and walks, is no more than a 10-minute stroll from the Launceston CBD, while Ben Lomond — Tasmania's major ski field and one of its most impressive mountains — is only an hour's drive from the city.

In the spectacular North-West, two hours is plenty of time to travel from hectares of tulips in bloom to the starting point of the world-famous Overland Track from Cradle Mountain to Lake St Clair.

Convict heritage and Tasmania's colonial past is also never far away. At Swansea, on the centre of the east coast, a walk around the headland beside Great Oyster Bay links Aboriginal and European history. Once the home of the local Aboriginal people who harvested shellfish from the rocks, it was also, early last century, the site of a barracks for the soldiers guarding the convict work parties.

The pace of life is even more tranquil on Tasmania's islands. King and Flinders islands in the Bass Strait have a charm all their own, and Bruny Island, less than half an hour from Hobart, is a popular weekend getaway.

Relax and take time to discover Australia's island state. There's no need to hurry or drive hundreds of kilometres — to do so would be to bypass much of Tasmania's charm.

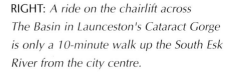

RIGHT: *A ride on the chairlift across The Basin in Launceston's Cataract Gorge is only a 10-minute walk up the South Esk River from the city centre.*

BELOW: *Free-ranging wallabies are a feature of several wildlife parks on the island, where there are no natural predators.*

## *Tasmanian politics*

ON THE POLITICAL FRONT, Tasmanians wryly observe that they have more politicians per capita than anywhere else in the country. The House of Assembly's 35 members are chosen to represent five electorates under the Hare–Clark system of proportional representation, allowing latitude for local knowledge and some voting across the parties to help elect the seven members for each seat. There is also a Legislative Council (19 members) which so far has survived pressure for reform or abolition. On top of that, the island sends five members to the House of Representatives and 12 senators to the Senate. More than 25 local councils (five in Hobart alone) complete the picture.

ABOVE: *Cloudy Bay on South Bruny Island from the historic lighthouse on Cape Bruny.*

LEFT: *The Tasmanian Tiger (or thylacine) is almost certainly extinct, but the Tasmanian Devil (pictured) still flourishes. A carrion eater and scavenger, it possesses very powerful jaws. All wildlife parks have Devils on show, some tame enough to be patted.*

LEFT: *Caves along the Franklin River provided shelter for Aborigines, some having been inhabited during the last Ice Age.*

*Hobart*

# HOBART

*Mountain and mellow charm*

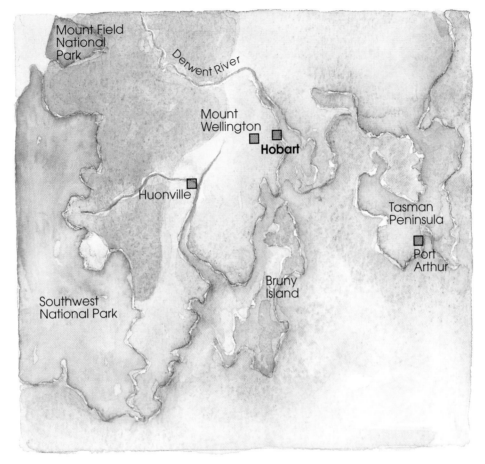

Hobart, Australia's second oldest city after Sydney, combines the mellow charm of its colonial heritage with a splendid natural setting sprawling along both sides of the River Derwent, with Mount Wellington providing an often-snowcapped backdrop. Founded at Sullivans Cove by Lieutenant David Collins in February 1804, after a settlement upstream at Risdon Cove was abandoned, the city today has a population of about 175 000.

The lifestyle is leisurely, with the Derwent and the D'Entrecasteaux Channel offering superb sailing waters, and wilderness extending almost to the doorstep. Sullivans Cove remains the heart of the city; now the restaurant precinct, it is

LEFT: *The hills above Sandy Bay provide sweeping views over Battery Point and the city.*
PREVIOUS PAGES: *Mt Wellington, 1270 metres above sea level, provides a breathtaking 360-degree view encompassing Hobart spread out below and the south-west wilderness.*

largely flat and windswept and can be extremely cold. If the road is closed by snow, head instead for Mount Nelson above the suburb of Sandy Bay. Once a semaphore station to Port Arthur, it has panoramic views of the city. Or visit the Royal Tasmanian Botanical Gardens, established in 1818. They are the second oldest in the nation and occupy a 13.5 hectare site overlooking the river.

Hobart is also the ideal base from which to visit much of southern Tasmania, including the Huon Valley and Channel, Bruny Island, the Tasman Peninsula and Port Arthur, the Derwent Valley and historic Richmond.

Bruny Island is only a 15-minute ferry ride from Kettering, which

also the site of the Taste of Tasmania which greets the first arrivals in the Sydney–Hobart Yacht Race.

The compact nature of the central business district makes Hobart an easy city to explore on foot. Soak up the port's atmosphere with its fishing fleet and punts selling fresh seafood and shellfish, yachts and ferries, freighters, and Antarctic exploration ships. Salamanca Place, at the southern end of the cove, is famous for its Saturday market but is also home to art galleries, bookshops, craft outlets, and restaurants.

Kelly's Steps lead up from Salamanca Place to Battery Point, Hobart's first suburb, largely unchanged from colonial times with street after

street of historic houses including Narryna, Australia's first folk museum.

Downtown Hobart's handsome sandstone streetscapes include almost 100 National Trust-classified buildings. One of Tasmania's treasures is the Theatre Royal in Campbell Street; built in 1837 it is the oldest theatre in Australia. The Allport Library and Museum, located in the State Library, features magnificent colonial furniture, silverware, china and art works.

A drive to the top of Mount Wellington (1270 metres) reveals a 360-degree view of the city, the East Coast, the south coast, Derwent Valley and part of the south-west wilderness. The summit is

is just south of Hobart and is rich in history — Cook and Bligh were among its early European visitors. It was also the birthplace of Truganini, the last of the full-blood Tasmanian Aborigines.

The Tasman Peninsula, south-east of Hobart, is best known as the site of Port Arthur, the colonial penal colony. The convict legacy still drives the local tourism industry, but bushwalking and the spectacular coastal scenery, along with fishing, diving and kayaking add to its appeal.

Mt Field, proclaimed in 1917 as the first of Tasmania's national parks, is little more than an hour from Hobart. In winter, the alpine area has southern Tasmania's only ski fields.

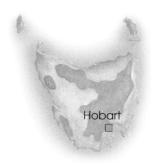

RIGHT: *Hobart's Salamanca market from the top of the grain silos. The Saturday market is one of the faces of Salamanca Place which also has become the centre of the city's arts and crafts, and the place for coffee and brunch.*

FAR RIGHT: *Rated one of the finest cool temperate gardens in the world, the Royal Tasmanian Botanical Gardens in Hobart — the second oldest botanical gardens in Australia — also feature an important sub-Antarctic collection.*

## Salamanca Market

The historic sandstone warehouses built from 1835 to 1860 provide a wonderful backdrop for Hobart's happening place — the Saturday Salamanca Market. The locals come to shop for fresh flowers, fruit and vegetables, and to socialise; the tourists to search for souvenirs, particularly quality art and craft; and both can pig out at the food stalls and the Salamanca cafes and restaurants.

The Market is very much Hobart's cosmopolitan heart and develops a buzz and a zip absent from the traditional Tasmanian lifestyle. A dozen or so mostly very talented buskers provide the entertainment with harpist George Callaghan a regular, along with a South American band, Arauco Libre, which is comprised mainly of Chilean refugees. Tasmania's newest community, the Hmong people from Laos, run a series of superb vegetable stalls, much frequented by enthusiasts of Asian cuisines. In all, some 300 stalls stretch from the original (1972) market in front of the warehouses up the hill to Davey Street. If you need a break from the crowd, take a stroll into St David's Park with its memorials to the first settlers. The market opens at 8.30am and continues into mid-afternoon.

After browsing the market scene, step inside some of the warehouses to discover several of the state's leading galleries and craft outlets. For families, the Dreamworld-owned and operated Antarctic Adventure centre will easily occupy two or three hours.

OPPOSITE: *Constitution Dock in Hobart plays host once a year to the Sydney-Hobart Yacht Race fleet. The race is a blue-water classic drawing competitors from throughout the world, and the yachts' arrival is the signal for the Hobart Summer Festival to swing into top gear.*

RIGHT: *Scores of spectacular craft farewelled the Tall Ships fleet as it left Hobart in February 1998.*

BELOW RIGHT: *Hobart's Tasman Bridge arcs over the Derwent, Mt Wellington looming in the background. A freighter moving upstream one night in 1976 hit the bridge — causing part of it to collapse — and sank.*

ABOVE: *Parliament House, Hobart, is situated close to the docks and was once the Customs House for the colony.*

RIGHT: *Bands playing in the handsome English-style rotunda in Hobart's St Davids Park must scare the ghosts from what was the colony's first cemetery.*

BELOW RIGHT: *A delightfully colonial atmosphere makes Battery Point, once home to merchants, mariners, fishermen and dock workers, one of Hobart's most sought after residential areas.*

TOP: *Abseiling from the grain silos in Salamanca Place adds excitement for summer visitors.*

ABOVE: *Hobart's Elizabeth Mall links Liverpool Street and Collins Street, the city's two main thoroughfares.*

RIGHT: *The tiny colonial cottages of Arthur Circus in Battery Point once housed dock workers employed to unload ships at nearby Salamanca Place. Today, a small garden in the middle is a playground for local children.*

FAR RIGHT: *The Boardwalk at Hobart's Wrest Point Hotel-Casino glows at dusk. Featuring a ferry and seaplane dock, it's also the perfect vantage point for the finish of the Sydney-Hobart Yacht Race.*

RIGHT: *In 1832, Peter Degraves established the imposing Cascade Brewery, Australia's oldest, beside a sparkling rivulet flowing down from Mt Wellington.*

BELOW: *Hobart's newest attraction, The Antarctic Adventure in Salamanca Place, offers visitors a taste of the icy south. The venture adds to the city's claims as the Antarctic gateway — Hobart already providores expedition ships from several nations, and is the home of the Australian Antarctic Division.*

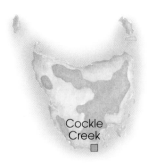

Cockle
Creek

RIGHT: *A lone penguin which waddled ashore at Cockle Creek, the southernmost settlement in Tasmania and starting point of the famous South Coast walking track.*

BELOW RIGHT: *A sculpture of a Southern Right whale at Cockle Creek – the creation of Tasmania's best known sculptor, Stephen Walker.*

FAR RIGHT: *Sunset at Cockle Creek in the far south of the Huon Valley, with the Hartz Mountains in the background. The blend of water and wilderness draws bushwalkers from all over the world.*

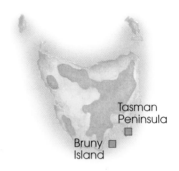

RIGHT: *Clouds over the Tasman Sea and Bruny Island's historic lighthouse combine to dramatic effect.*

OPPOSITE: *The Tasman Peninsula, site of the Port Arthur ruins, also offers spectacular clifftop walks.*

BELOW: *An isthmus joins Courts Island to Cape Bruny.*

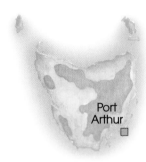

Port
Arthur

RIGHT: *Badly damaged by fire last century, the convict-built church at the Port Arthur Historic Site was used in 1997 for an anniversary service in memory of the victims of the 1996 Port Arthur massacre.*

FAR RIGHT: *The picturesque ruins of the penitentiary at Port Arthur stand witness to the 12 500 convicts who served time there between 1830 and 1877.*

BELOW: *The first light of dawn catches the tessellated pavement at Eaglehawk Neck on the Tasman Peninsula.*

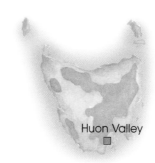

Huon Valley

LEFT: *Traditional boat-building skills have been revived at the School of Wooden Boatbuilding at Franklin, on the Huon River.*

RIGHT: *Tasmania's prize timber, Huon pine, was first found along the banks of the tranquil Huon River.*

BELOW: *New varieties of apples and a push into Asian markets revived Tasmania's famous apple growing industry after the crippling blow it suffered when the United Kingdom entered the European Common Market in 1973.*

Mount Field
National Park

**FAR RIGHT:** *Russell Falls in the Mt Field National Park. The track to the 40-metre falls is accessible by wheelchair, and the park itself is about 35 minutes' drive from New Norfolk.*

**RIGHT:** *The Swamp Gum* (Eucalyptus regnans) *is the tallest flowering plant in the world and can grow to 100 metres in height. Known as Tasmanian oak, it is used for constructing houses and furniture.*

**BELOW RIGHT:** *The echidna, or spiny anteater, is relatively common throughout Tasmania. The ant-eaters and the platypus are the only furred animals which lay eggs.*

# The Heritage Highway

# THE HERITAGE HIGHWAY

*The road to the past*

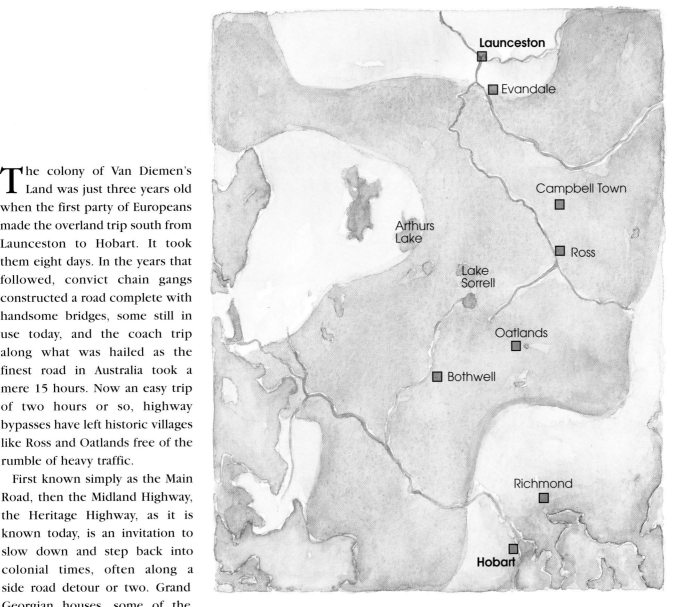

Launceston

Evandale

Campbell Town

Arthurs Lake

Ross

Lake Sorrell

Oatlands

Bothwell

Richmond

Hobart

The colony of Van Diemen's Land was just three years old when the first party of Europeans made the overland trip south from Launceston to Hobart. It took them eight days. In the years that followed, convict chain gangs constructed a road complete with handsome bridges, some still in use today, and the coach trip along what was hailed as the finest road in Australia took a mere 15 hours. Now an easy trip of two hours or so, highway bypasses have left historic villages like Ross and Oatlands free of the rumble of heavy traffic.

First known simply as the Main Road, then the Midland Highway, the Heritage Highway, as it is known today, is an invitation to slow down and step back into colonial times, often along a side road detour or two. Grand Georgian houses, some of the nation's oldest farming properties, village fairs, lakes and streams in which to fish, and cottage and farm accommodation can all be found along the way.

In the north, the historic experience begins at Evandale, less than five kilometres from Launceston airport. Wander along charming streetscapes which have changed little in well over a century, or among the extensive formal gardens and parklands of Clarendon, a splendid National Trust property.

On the other side of the highway find Longford (c. 1813), complete with village green and, close by, Woolmer's Estate — a virtual time capsule of European settlement with original furnishings and memorabilia. Campbell Town, once an important garrison on the highway, has a convict-built bridge and dozens of buildings dating back to the 1830s, but it is Ross, 10 kilometres further south, which best evokes the colonial era.

The main street is delightful with its Georgian buildings and avenue of English elms, and the magnificent bridge, built by convicts in 1836, is an icon of the Tasmanian tourist industry.

Another former garrison town, Oatlands is reckoned to have the largest number of Georgian-era buildings in Australia — the main street alone has more than 80! The town landmark, the National Trust-registered Callington Mill was established as a flour mill in 1837. The windmill has been recently restored and guided ghost tours depart nightly.

Also worth the diversion, especially if you're a keen angler, is Lake Sorrell, on the Central Plateau west of the highway and Bothwell, a charming village founded by Scots settlers in the 1820s, and is now best known as a trout-fishing centre.

Finally, before driving into Hobart, take a detour off the Heritage Highway route to Richmond, one of Tasmania's most delightful historic villages and an important arts and craft centre.

OPPOSITE: *Not strictly on the Heritage Highway, Richmond — a quaint historic village just north of Hobart — is home to many shops and galleries and the Richmond Arms Hotel.*
PREVIOUS PAGES: *Convict stonemason Daniel Herbert 's carvings make Ross Bridge unique.*

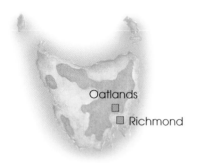

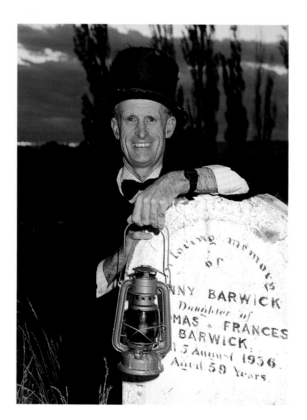

FAR RIGHT: *The Callington Mill at Oatlands, restored as a bicentenary project and now open for inspection, was constructed in 1837 to grind grain and is one of only a few remaining in Australia from that time.*

TOP RIGHT: *Old Hobart Town — a scale model attraction at historic Richmond village — shows Hobart Town as it was in the 1820s. Based on early colonial records, the model serves as an excellent introduction to a stroll around the real thing!*

MIDDLE RIGHT: *The Richmond Gaol, complete with flogging yard and work rooms, remains virtually unchanged from when it was first built in 1825.*

BOTTOM RIGHT: *Oatlands ghost tour guide Peter Fielding dresses for the occasion in the historic Midlands township dating from the 1830s.*

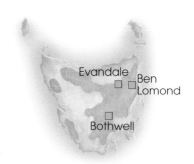

Evandale  Ben
           Lomond

Bothwell

RIGHT: *Widely regarded as the finest Georgian mansion in the nation, Clarendon House at Nile, near Evandale, was built in 1838 and is among Tasmania's great colonial treasures.*

BELOW RIGHT: *Ben Lomond, site of the state's main skiing area, looms on the horizon as sheep graze peacefully just off the Highway.*

BELOW: *Settled in 1813, Longford, in northern Tasmania, is known for its convict-built buildings and surrounding English-style countryside with farming properties dating back to the 1820s.*

TOP: *Bothwell, in the Central Highlands, features more than 50 historic buildings as well as Australia's first golf course.*

ABOVE: *Penny farthing championships are held in Evandale in February every year — competitors come from as far away as the US and the UK.*

RIGHT: *Richmond Bridge and St Johns Roman Catholic Church combine to produce a charming vision of old English countryside. The bridge is Australia's oldest, built by convicts between 1832 and 1835, while St Johns is the oldest Catholic church in the nation.*

OPPOSITE: *The stark beauty of Arthurs Lake in the Central Highlands — one of scores of lakes in the highlands, all of which attract trout fishermen from throughout Australia and beyond.*

RIGHT: *Lake Sorell is another of the lakes that make Tasmania an angler's paradise. Indeed, fishing may well be the state's most popular recreation as Tasmania offers the world's best wild trout fishing.*

BELOW: *Distinctive fishing shacks line the shores of Lake Sorell — the shack tradition is firmly entrenched, and the region's often sudden and severe changes of weather make such shelter very important.*

BELOW RIGHT: *An angler proudly displays his catch. This fine brown trout is a tribute to both his skill and the far-sighted officials who, in 1864, established the first trout hatchery in the Southern Hemisphere at Plenty, near New Norfolk.*

Arthur's Lake

Lake Sorell

## Trout fishing

The trout in Tasmania are no easier to catch than anywhere else, but what adds to the experience is that the island is reckoned by some anglers to offer the best wild trout fishing in the world. The first trout in the Southern Hemisphere were introduced to Tasmania in 1864, along with salmon. The salmon failed but the trout thrived, and their progeny were later used to stock mainland and New Zealand waters.

Today, no place in Tasmania is more than an hour from wonderful angling opportunities, from coastal rivers and streams to highland lakes and tarns. Wilderness settings and unpolluted waters add to the appeal, and expert guides are available. Two bonuses for fly fishermen are being able to 'tail' the trout when they swim into very shallow water to feed and 'polaroiding', the summer-time thrill of using sunglasses to spot trout cruising in the shallows and then trying to tempt them to take a lure.

The season runs from the August until the end of April. The Salmon Ponds hatchery at Plenty, where it all began in 1864, is open seven days a week and features a Museum of Trout Fishing in the cottage built for the first superintendant in 1865. You are welcome to handfeed the hundreds of trout and salmon in the display ponds.

An incentive for anglers fishing southern coastal waters, rivers and streams, especially in the Huon and Derwent, is the large numbers of Atlantic salmon which have escaped from farming pens.

# Launceston

# LAUNCESTON

*From streetscapes to snowfields*

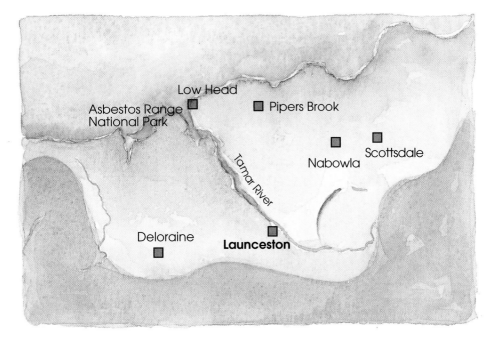

Asbestos Range
National Park

Low Head

Pipers Brook

Tamar River

Nabowla

Scottsdale

Deloraine

**Launceston**

LEFT: *Bridestowe Estate Lavender Farm at Nabowla, north-east of Launceston, where oil is produced for the international perfume industry.*

PREVIOUS PAGES: *Launceston, Tasmania's second largest city, spreads below Mt Barrow.*

Launceston is Australia's third oldest city and, although only a year younger than Hobart, has a character all its own, with grand Victorian streetscapes and the great natural attraction of the nearby Cataract Gorge. Situated on the Tamar River 64 kilometres upstream from where the Tamar enters Bass Strait, Launceston spreads across wide valleys and has superb mountain backdrops, most notably Ben Lomond, Mount Arthur and Mount Barrow.

The city's proudest boast is that it was from here that John Batman sailed in 1835 to found Melbourne. The Batman Fawkner Inn, where the meeting was held which led to the decision, is still trading and contains some mementos of Melbourne's beginnings. The Queen Victoria Museum & Art Gallery is a handsome building and its collection includes some fine colonial paintings. Also of interest is the Chinese joss house which once stood in the main street of the north-east tin-mining town, Weldborough.

Where the South Esk River flows through the gorge to join the Tamar there are good walking tracks, a suspension bridge and a chairlift. The area is also a wildlife reserve and in summer is a venue for concerts. City Park, established in the 1820s, is one of Launceston's great treasures and includes a conservatory, and the children's favourite — a monkey island populated by rhesus monkeys. Just outside the park, the Design Centre of Tasmania presents the best of Tasmanian crafts, especially furniture, and is open seven days a week. Several excellent restaurants, and the proximity of the Tamar Valley vineyards, mix well with the appeal of Launceston's bustling city heart.

The development of cool climate wines has moved apace since the 1980s, and the Tamar River valley is one of Tasmania's most important wine-producing regions. Follow the wine route along both sides of the valley, or take a river cruise or float plane flight; both are available from the centre of the city.

Low Head, at the mouth of the river on its eastern side, is one of Australia's most important historic precincts. It was here that Bass and Flinders spent time in 1798 en route to circum-navigating the state. The pilot station is Australia's oldest continually operating station and also includes a maritime museum. Low Head has another attraction — fairy penguin colonies which can be seen coming ashore each evening.

Like most areas in Tasmania, Launceston is within easy reach of the natural environment. Ben Lomond, only an hour from the city, is known as Tasmania's best skiing area, and a popular summer destination as well. The Asbestos Range National Park, which runs along the coast from near the west bank of the Tamar, is a prime area in which to see the native fauna.

Deloraine, midway between Launceston and Devonport, sits at the base of the Great Western Tiers and is a popular bushwalking centre. It is a classified historic town and each year in late October or early November stages a four-day craft fair — Australia's largest. Beautiful riverside walks, and the fact that it is now bypassed by the highway, enhance its appeal. The Mole Creek Caves are close by and visitors can explore some of the fascinating limestone formations.

A pleasant day can also be spent east of Launceston, touring the vineyards in the Pipers Brook region and visiting the Bridestowe Estate Lavender Farm at Nabowla, the largest in the Southern Hemisphere. The estate is in full bloom by early December when the harvest begins. While in the area, call in at the Walker Rhododendron Reserve at Lalla. Some of the varieties are more than 60 years old and tower six metres. The Hollybank Forest Reserve, with its oaks, ash, pines and eucalypts, is a delightful picnic spot and is on the approach to Lilydale.

Launceston

RIGHT: *A pagoda nestles amongst spring flowers in Launceston's Cataract Gorge, a mix of parklands, swimming areas and wilderness only 10 minutes from the heart of the city.*

FAR RIGHT: *The elegant Launceston paddle-steamer, Lady Stelfox, cruises up and down the Tamar River and through the Cataract Gorge every day.*

BELOW: *A bustling pedestrian mall in central Launceston reveals how successful the plan to enhance the appeal of the city has been.*

OPPOSITE: *Tasmania's small but high quality wine industry, centred on the Tamar Valley and the adjacent Pipers Brook region, has attracted investment from interstate and French wine interests. Here, Geoff Clifford of Cliff House Vineyard in the Tamar Valley, works hard on his vines.*

RIGHT: *The Westbury Maze is just one of the attractions of the charming town of Westbury beside the Bass Highway. About 35 kilometres from Launceston, Westbury also boasts a genuine village green.*

BELOW FAR RIGHT: *The Trowunna Wildlife Park at Mole Creek, open throughout the year, allows visitors a glimpse of native animals, such as this wombat, in a natural setting.*

MIDDLE RIGHT: *A browse through the antique shops in the area around Deloraine, about halfway between Launceston and Devonport, can still result in an attractive bargain or two.*

BOTTOM RIGHT: *The historic town of Deloraine, on the Meander River, is now bypassed by the main highway, adding to the pleasure of strolling or picnicing in the riverside park.*

Deloraine ☐☐ ☐ Tamar Valley
Westbury

## Wine

Tasmania's small but fast-expanding wine industry is coming under increasing notice for its fine quality cool-climate wines. Commercial production began in the mid-1970s, and in recent years there has been investment in vineyards from French interests. Chardonnay and pinot noir are particularly well-suited to the Tasmanian environment, and there are also some excellent cabernet sauvignons.

In the past 10 years vineyard plantings have increased from 42 hectares to more than 400 hectares, and there are more than 20 cellar door outlets.

The key vineyard areas are the west bank of the Tamar in the north and the Pipers Brook region to the east of Launceston. Other wine-producing areas are the East Coast, Derwent Valley, Coal River Valley (near Richmond), the Huon and Hobart. Moorilla Estate, in a riverside setting in Hobart's northern suburbs, was the first commercial vineyard in the state and includes an award-winning restaurant specialising in Tasmanian food.

In all, Tasmania's winemakers produce about 1.7 million bottles annually, half of which is sold in the state. They plan to quadruple the present crop of some 2000 tonnes by the year 2007 and lift cellar door sales to more than $60 million. But, even with this expansion, Tasmania will remain a very small — though quality — element in the Australian wine scene.

Low Head

Asbestos Range
National Park

**LEFT:** *The historic Low Head lighthouse at the mouth of the Tamar River, built in 1888, offers superb views up and down the coast.*

**RIGHT:** *Sweeping pink fields of opium poppies can be seen throughout Tasmania — the only state in Australia permitted to grow the poppies commercially.*

**BELOW:** *Wallabies grazing in the Asbestos Range National Park.*

# The West

# THE WEST

*A world of wilderness*

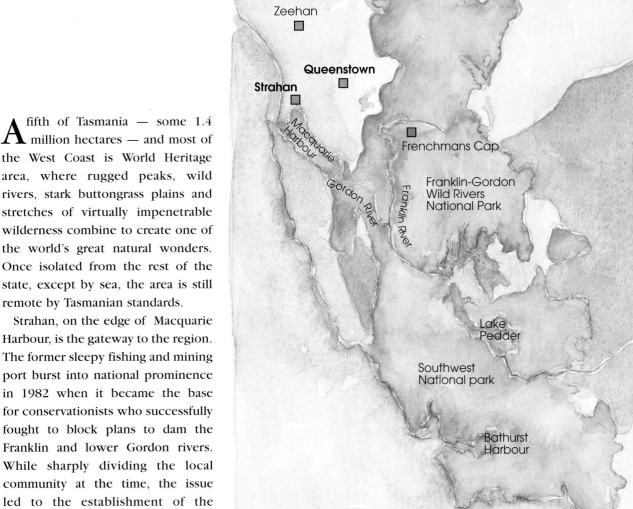

Zeehan

**Queenstown**

**Strahan**

Macquarie Harbour

Gordon River

Frenchmans Cap

Franklin River

Franklin-Gordon
Wild Rivers
National Park

Lake
Pedder

Southwest
National park

Bathurst
Harbour

A fifth of Tasmania — some 1.4 million hectares — and most of the West Coast is World Heritage area, where rugged peaks, wild rivers, stark buttongrass plains and stretches of virtually impenetrable wilderness combine to create one of the world's great natural wonders. Once isolated from the rest of the state, except by sea, the area is still remote by Tasmanian standards.

Strahan, on the edge of Macquarie Harbour, is the gateway to the region. The former sleepy fishing and mining port burst into national prominence in 1982 when it became the base for conservationists who successfully fought to block plans to dam the Franklin and lower Gordon rivers. While sharply dividing the local community at the time, the issue led to the establishment of the ecotourism industry on which the town thrives today.

The Strahan Visitor Centre, part interpretative centre, part information centre, carries a strong record of the conservation battle of the 1980s and introduces the region's natural environment. The centre also outlines the history of the West Coast, beginning with Aboriginal occupation over a period of 35 000 years and continuing with the arrival of the first Europeans — the convicts and guards sent in 1821 to Macquarie Harbour to harvest Huon pine.

LEFT: *Remote and beautiful, Bathurst Harbour lies deep in heart of the south-west.*
PREVIOUS PAGES: *Swathed in clouds, the Frankland Range rises dramatically behind the moody stillness of Lake Pedder in the rugged South-West National Park.*

Accessing the wilderness from Strahan can be as simple as taking a leisurely half-hour stroll from the wharf area into dense rainforest. A more spectacular approach is by float plane from the harbour — an 80-minute trip including a landing on the beautiful Gordon River and a flight over the World Heritage area. Other options include a spectacular helicopter flight into a magnificent Huon pine forest or a cruise across Macquarie Harbour and up the Gordon River.

Ocean Beach, just outside Strahan is, at 33 kilometres, Tasmania's longest beach and a place of awesome beauty. On summer evenings, thousands of muttonbirds returning to their rookeries fill the sky, and. platypus can sometimes be seen in the streams cutting across the beach.

Queenstown, 40 kilometres north-east of Strahan, is the coast's major town and remains an important copper mining centre. Its near-lunar hillsides — the legacy of timber-felling, mining pollution and heavy rainfall — still retain a curious beauty, but nature is gradually restoring the landscape, assisted by an end to past mining practices. Visitors in Queenstown can make an extraordinary underground tour to a point 650 metres below the surface to watch actual mining operations. Despite its environmental degradation, the town is close to many areas of pristine beauty, such as the Nelson Falls nature walk just off the Lyell Highway, 25 minutes on the Hobart side of the town.

Just north of Queenstown lies Zeehan, known as 'Silver City' after the discovery of silver and lead in the area in 1882. Handsome buildings along the main street hint at the long-gone boom days.

Strahan

RIGHT: *Cruise boats pack the jetty at the once sleepy fishing port of Strahan, on Macquarie Harbour.*

BOTTOM: *Atlantic salmon farming in Macquarie Harbour is part of the growing aquaculture industry.*

BELOW: *Wide verandahs line Strahan's main street, quiet as visitors spend the day out in the wilderness.*

## Tasmanian food

The most startling change about Tasmania in the past 20 years is its emergence as a producer of quality foodstuffs. Just as important to the visitor and locals alike is that the restaurant scene, particularly in Hobart and Launceston, has begun to focus strongly on the bounty.

Aquaculture is one industry to benefit from the unpolluted waters with oyster farms delivering some 3.5 million dozen oysters each year. And the Atlantic salmon industry, little more than a decade old, is on track to harvest close to 5000 tonnes a year by the turn of the century. Sea-raised rainbow trout are another speciality. Although rising costs are forcing rock lobster beyond the reach of most diners, the range of scale fish landed from off the coast is adequate compensation. Try the trevalla or flounder as an example.

Tasmania's image as the 'apple isle' has grown in recent times with replantings to target Asian markets. From March to May the orchards have roadside stalls of fresh-picked fruit. And from December to May also look for berry fruit.

It's worth remembering that the state is a major vegetable producer, accounting for a quarter of the nation's potatoes. There's none better than the local favourite, the 'pinkeye', a sweet golden potato best eaten boiled with a dab of butter.

Cheese is another bonus, from the famous King Island brie to traditional cheddars and goats' cheese from Bothwell.

Macquarie
Harbour □

TOP: *John 'Jack' Farrell rows his boat across Macquarie Harbour at Strahan on the West Coast.*

RIGHT: *Skippers in the days of sail were sometimes forced, in wild weather, to return to Hobart rather than risk Hell's Gates, the narrow and dangerous entrance to Macquarie Harbour.*

ABOVE: *Thousands of muttonbirds (short-tailed shearwaters) at Ocean Beach, near Strahan, migrate from Siberia each year to breed among the dunes.*

Gordon River

LEFT: *Tranquil in the early morning light, the Gordon River can quickly become a foaming torrent, rising by several metres after rainfall upstream.*

RIGHT: *The gnarled shape of this ancient Huon pine beside the Gordon River probably saved it from loggers last century, when prime timber was abundant. Pines such as these can live for thousands of years.*

BELOW: *A startled Tasmanian green tree frog clings to reeds in a south-west swamp at midnight. After taking the shot, the photographer noticed a tiger snake observing him from half a metre away!*

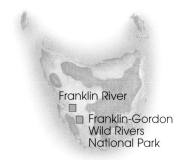

Franklin River
☐ Franklin-Gordon
Wild Rivers
National Park

LEFT: *The spectacular Bingham's Arch Cave on the Franklin River is one of a series in the south-west wilderness. Some show evidence of Aboriginal occupation dating back 30 000 years.*

RIGHT: *Nelson Falls, just off the Lyell Highway, 25 minutes' drive east of Queenstown, is an easy 20-minute return walk through rainforest at the edge of the Franklin-Gordon Wild Rivers National Park.*

BELOW: *The pandani heath, endemic to Tasmania, is generally found in rainforest as part of the understorey, and is the world's tallest flowering heath.*

Lake Pedder

RIGHT: *Lake Pedder, flooded by the Hydro-Electric Commission in 1972, is now many times its original size and up to 300 metres deep. While the loss of the original lake and its magnificent white sand beach is lamented by many, the new lake's excellent trout fishing draws anglers from around Australia.*

FAR RIGHT: *Morning mist and reflections greet visitors at Heritage Landing on the Gordon River, the turnaround point for cruises from Strahan and a chance for tourists to step into the rainforest.*

BELOW RIGHT: *The 140-metre-high Gordon Dam created Lake Gordon as part of Tasmania's biggest hydro-electric scheme. Tours can be made of the underground power station, not far from Lake Pedder.*

RIGHT: *Sarah Island, in Macquarie Harbour, once Tasmania's most savage penal settlement, offers visitors a brush with its brutal history.*

BELOW RIGHT: *A flight along the rugged West Coast gives an idea why it was so dangerous to early sailing ships. Even today, the coast is no stranger to tragedy as small boats work the rich fishing grounds offshore.*

BELOW: *Whitewater rafting on the Franklin River is one of Tasmania's most adventurous wilderness experiences. A trip can take from 8 to 14 days and is not for the faint-hearted.*

TOP: *Park rangers work on the track to Frenchmans Cap in the Franklin-Gordon Wild Rivers National Park — the walk takes four to five days and should be attempted only by experienced bushwalkers.*

RIGHT: *The summit of Frenchmans Cap, 1443 metres high and often snowcapped well into summer, affords spectacular views across the south-west wilderness.*

ABOVE: *This orange bellied parrot — a threatened species once thought to be extinct — was spotted at Birchs Inlet in the Wild Rivers National Park.*

Queenstown

RIGHT TOP: *The narrow, winding road and bare hills between Queenstown and Gormanston are a stark contrast to the great natural wilderness in the region.*

FAR RIGHT: *Morning mist lifts from the West Coast town of Queenstown and its surrounding hills. Copper mining, begun at Mt Lyell in the 1890s, and the smelting which followed it, helped produce an almost lunar landscape, only now being regenerated.*

RIGHT MIDDLE: *Orr Street, Queenstown's main street, is quiet these days but there are echoes of the boom days earlier this century.*

RIGHT BOTTOM: *An underground miner at Pasminco's Rosebery mine. More than 120 years after the West Coast's mining riches were first revealed, the search for more ore bodies continues throughout the region.*

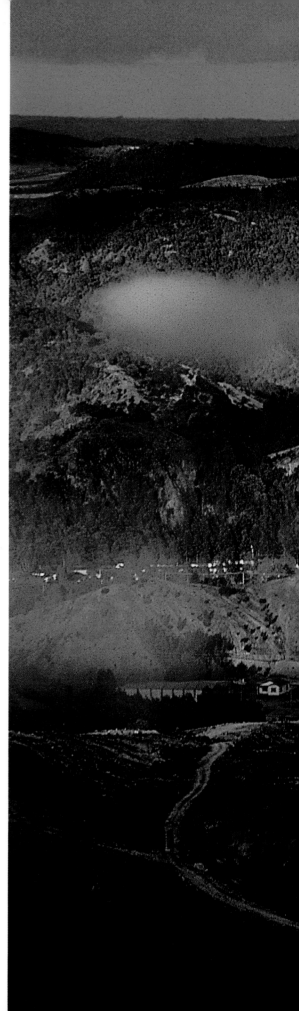

The East

# THE EAST

*A coastal escape*

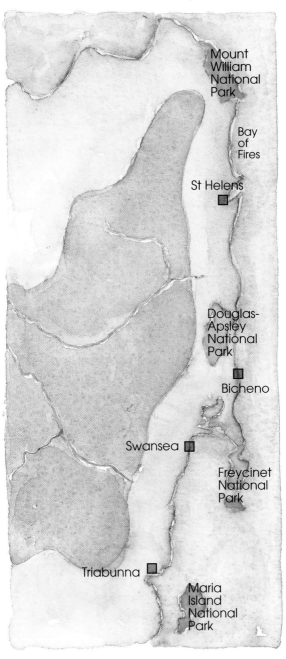

The East Coast is laidback and relaxed even by Tasmanian standards. Its mild climate, good fishing and superb unspoiled beaches make it a year-round destination for local holidaymakers. Four national parks from Mount William in the far north-east to Maria Island in the south, and some of the finest temperate dive waters in the world add to its attractions.

The region is dotted with small towns, each with its own particular charm and natural attractions. Orford, on the southern end of the coast and less than an hour from Hobart, is the departure point for the ferry to Maria Island, once a major convict settlement. The old penitentiary is now used as bunkhouse accommodation, and there is also a campground. With no transport on the island and no predators, the wildlife — particularly the wallabies — is unfazed by visitors.

The most spectacular view on the Tasman Highway — across Great Oyster Bay to the Freycinet Peninsula — can be found on the southern approach to Swansea. Swansea itself was founded in the 1820s and many fine buildings remain from the middle of the last century and even earlier, including a three-storey general store dating back to 1838. For an introduction to the district's history, visit the restored Swansea Bark Mill and its museum — the machinery set up in 1885 to crush wattle bark for tanning still clanks away. The bayside walk around Waterloo Point skirts muttonbird rookeries and offers a fine view of the ever-changing colours of the Freycinet Peninsula as well as the chance to spot dolphins and the occasional migratory whale. Much of the point

LEFT: *The unusual 'painted cliffs' of Maria Island NP.*
PREVIOUS PAGES: *Spectacular Wineglass Bay on the Freycinet Peninsula, from the summit of Mount Amos.*

itself is an Aboriginal midden, the vast mound of shells and other refuse standing as evidence of occupation over several thousand years.

The Freycinet National Park and its breathtaking Wineglass Bay, are among Tasmania's best known tourism icons. Freycinet Lodge, in the park itself, is a national ecotourism award-winner and is merged sensitively into the park surrounds. Take the time to climb up to the lookout; the view of Wineglass Bay alone is worth it. Coles Bay, with its backdrop of pink granite peaks, is a pretty fishing port and holiday centre with a good range of accommodation.

To the north of Freycinet is Bicheno, first visited around 1803 by whalers and sealers. These days the offshore waters are a marine park and a mecca for divers. There are fairy penguin rookeries nearby, and seals occasionally bask on rocks along quiet stretches of beach. As with most of the East Coast the Bicheno hinterland also has plenty to offer. The Douglas Apsley National Park is easily accessible and features a charming riverside picnic spot as well as an interesting short walk to a lookout point.

St Helens, on the shores of the vast and almost landlocked Georges Bay, is the coast's most important fishing port with crayfish and giant king crabs among the harvest. The bay itself provides fine recreational fishing, and charter operators run game fishing trips offshore. The St Helens History Room is an excellent source of information on the district. The coastal sand dunes are magnificent and the beaches at Binalong Bay and Scamander are among the best in the state. A short drive inland leads to Pyengana with its 'Pub in the Paddock' and the nearby St Columba Falls. Also visit the Pyengana cheese factory, renowned for its traditional cheddars.

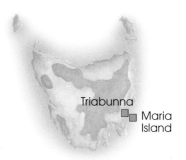

Triabunna
Maria
Island

**BELOW:** *Woodchips are loaded at Triabunna on the East Coast — woodchip exports to Japan is a sensitive issue but it provides employment for small communities.*

**BELOW RIGHT:** *Mount Maria, at 700 metres the highest point on Maria Island, provides a glorious view south over the isthmus.*

**BOTTOM:** *The giant equipment used in the timber industry today means unloading logs at the Triabunna mill is not quite as hard as it used to be.*

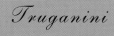

### Truganini

Truganini, the last of the Tasmanian Aboriginal people, died in Hobart on 8 May 1876, aged 64, but it was to be another 100 years before she was finally laid to rest. Born on Bruny Island, Truganini helped George Augustus Robinson to gather the remaining Aboriginal people together during the 1830s and was transferred with them to Flinders Island.

In 1847 the survivors, including Truganini, were moved to Oyster Cove, near Hobart. Oyster Cove was within sight of her birthplace and she was able to visit it. Her wish was to be buried in the D'Entrecasteaux Channel, beside Bruny Island, but she feared her body would be used for scientific research as had happened earlier with William Lanne, the last full-blood male Aborigine. Her fears were well founded as the Royal Society in Hobart asked the government for her body the day after her death, describing it as a valuable scientific specimen. The request was refused and she was buried near the chapel in the female prison at South Hobart.

Two years later, the body was exhumed and her skeleton acquired by the society. It was on display in the Tasmanian Museum & Art Gallery from 1904–1947, before being stored in the vaults. Moves by the Tasmanian Aboriginal community for her skeleton to be cremated and her ashes scattered on the waters of the D'Entrecasteaux Channel finally succeeded, and the ceremony was held on 1 May 1976.

ABOVE: *Day passes for visitors to Maria Island are available from the National Parks Office located in an historic building near the ferry jetty.*

RIGHT: *The climb up the quaintly named Bishop and Clerk on the north-eastern side of Maria Island, provides stunning views of the Freycinet Peninsula.*

Freycinet
National Park

**FAR RIGHT:** *The glorious stretch of the Friendly Beaches near Coles Bay is approached through heathlands and wildflowers (in season), and is part of the Freycinet National Park.*

**RIGHT TOP:** *There is nothing quite like windsurfing at Coles Bay on Freycinet Peninsula, the red granite peaks of the Hazards rising in the background.*

**RIGHT MIDDLE:** *A crayfishing boat returns to port at sunset·— the East Coast waters still produce some excellent catches, but the once-humble cray is now often priced beyond most people's reach, such is the demand from Asian markets.*

**RIGHT BOTTOM:** *This young Pacific gull at Freycinet is just one of the rich variety of native bird species that attracts ornithologists to the national park.*

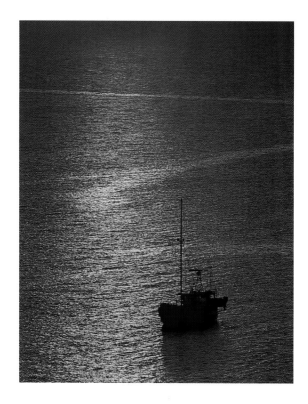

Bay of Fires
St Helens

RIGHT: *Crayfish are a prime catch of the local fishing fleet at St Helens, the main fishing port on the East Coast. Much of the catch, including king crabs from the edge of the continental shelf, is flown from the local airfield to Sydney and Melbourne markets.*

FAR RIGHT: *Low tide in the Bay of Fires, north of Binalong Bay on the East Coast, exposes bull kelp clinging to the rocks. The valuable seaweed is common along the coast.*

BELOW RIGHT: *Fishing boats and pleasure craft crowd Binalong Bay — a holiday and retirement community with excellent beaches and a laidback lifestyle just 10 kilometres north of St Helens.*

Bicheno

RIGHT: *Lichen-encrusted boulders stand sentinel at the Bay of Fires; the area gained its name from the early sightings of fires lit by local Aborigines.*

FAR RIGHT: *Bicheno, one of the East Coast's main holiday centres, spreads out below Whalers Hill. The whaling and sealing which brought the first Europeans to the area in the early 1800s is long gone, and today the offshore waters are a marine reserve, and the town makes its living from tourism.*

BELOW: *Cattle graze peacefully on a river flat beside the Apsley River near Bicheno.*

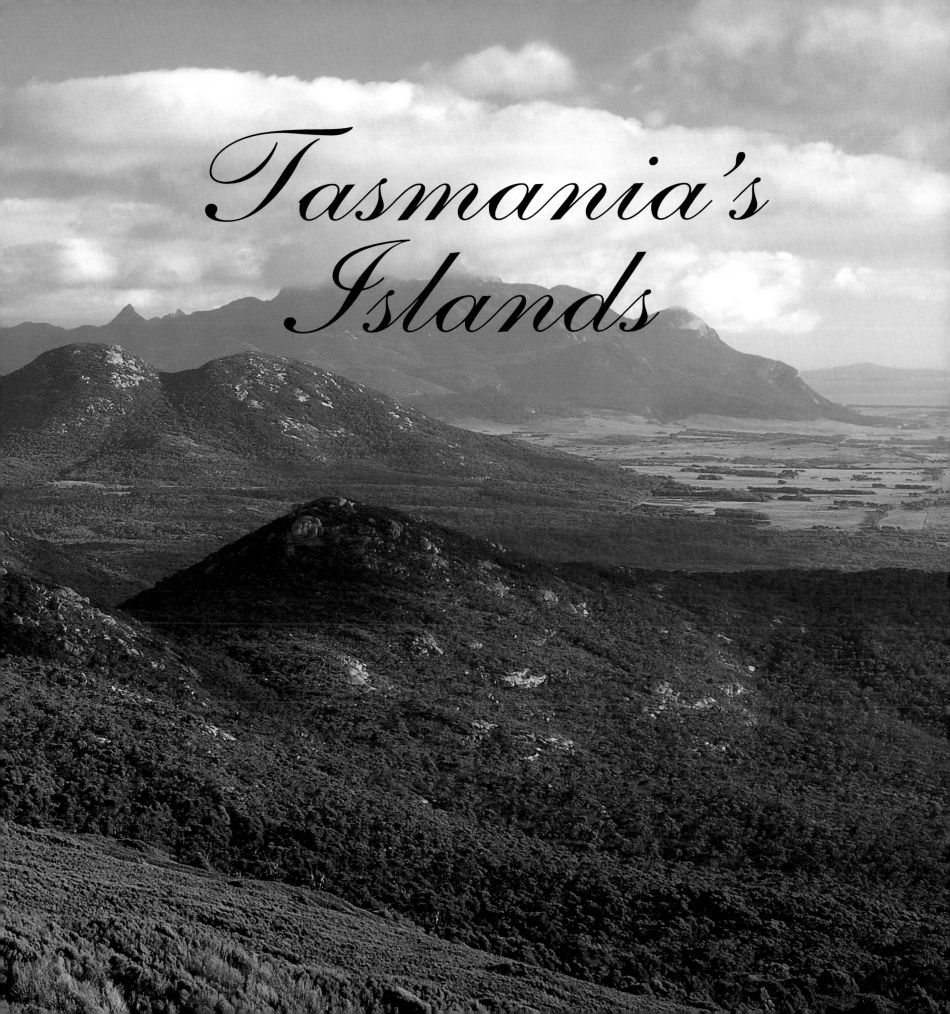

# Tasmania's Islands

# TASMANIA'S ISLANDS

*In the wake of Bass and Flinders*

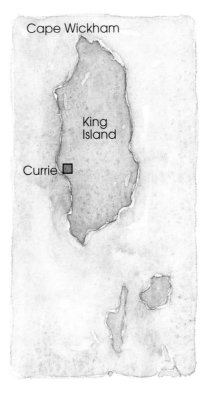

Until about 12 000 years ago Tasmania was joined to the Australian mainland, but the flooding of the Bass Plain following the last Ice Age severed that direct link, leaving as reminders the Bass Strait islands. The largest, King Island and Flinders Island — guarding the western and eastern ends of the 230km-wide strait — are as diverse as Tasmania itself. Certainly they have little in common, save for the slow and relaxed pace of life. Air travel has lessened the isolation and opened both to tourism.

King Island, approximately 65 kilometres long and 25 kilometres wide is, in modern times, best known for dairying and crayfish, and produces renowned cream and high-quality cheeses. Surprisingly, seaweed has been harvested commercially since the 1970s and is worth some $2 million a year to the island's economy. But the waters around King Island aren't always subdued — they have swallowed at least 50 wrecks. The worst, in 1845, claimed 399 lives. The historic lighthouses are a legacy of that era and the most northerly one, Cape Wickham, is Australia's biggest. The rocky coastline also offers many splendid beaches and, of course, great diving around various wreck sites.

Trail riding, beach walks, bushwalks and mountain biking are among the island's most popular activities, along with the seafood, cheese, and beef tasting for which it is famous. Coach tours operate to both ends of the island

LEFT: *Frank Cullen, a kelp harvester, visits a King Island beach strewn with bull kelp — a source of the alginates used for thickening sauces, cosmetics and detergents.*
PREVIOUS PAGES: *The Darling Range on Flinders Island stretches towards Mt Strzelecki.*

and the fairy penguin rookery near Currie can be visited each evening. Access to the island is by air from either Melbourne or the North-West Coast of Tasmania.

Flinders Island, largest of the Furneaux group, is about the same size as King Island and is part of the ancient land bridge which once linked Tasmania to the mainland. The island was named after Matthew Flinders who led a rescue mission there in 1798 to collect the survivors of the *Sydney Cove* — wrecked between Cape Barren Island and Clarke Island in 1797. The weather is surprisingly mild and the blend of beaches, farmlands, coastal heath and granite peaks makes it one of Tasmania's very special places.

Flinders Island was once home to tens of thousands of seals which were slaughtered by sealers who were also believed to have been

responsible for some of the scores of shipwrecks by using false lights to lure craft onto rocks. The other tragic element to the island's history is the relocation of the last full-blood Tasmanian Aboriginal people to a settlement at Wybalena where most of them died. The few who survived were eventually transferred to Oyster Cove, near Hobart. The historic site includes a graveyard and a chapel.

Flinders Island's two main centres are Whitemark and the fishing port of Lady Barron overlooking Franklin Sound. Throughout the summer and into autumn an evening cruise operates from Lady Barron to see vast flocks of muttonbirds (short-tailed shearwaters) returning to their rookeries at dusk.

Near the tip of the western side of the island is Killiecrankie Bay, a glorious beach with a small crayfishing fleet moored offshore. It's also the location of the Killiecrankie 'diamonds' which are actually topaz. They can be found by digging in the sand on the beaches, but the local expert, a fisherman, uses a small pump to dredge them from the bottom of the bay.

Mount Strezlecki, at 756 metres, is the highest point on Flinders Island. It offers good rock climbing and stunning views of the other islands in the Furneaux group. Flinders has regular air services from Melbourne and Sale in Victoria and from Launceston.

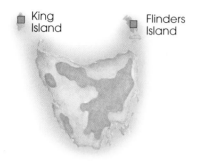

King Island    Flinders Island

RIGHT: *Crayfishing boats sheltering in Currie Harbour on King Island from a Bass Strait storm.*

OPPOSITE LEFT TOP: *Dairy cattle graze on King Island — superb cheeses and cream, as well as high quality beef and seafood, have made King Island a gourmet's paradise.*

OPPOSITE LEFT MIDDLE: *A Cape Barren Goose makes itself at home on Flinders Island. Once threatened with extinction, the bird is now so prolific it's a source of frustration to farmers because of its impact on crops and feed.*

OPPOSITE LEFT BOTTOM: *The remains of a 7000-year-old calcified forest form bizarre skeletal shapes near the southern tip of King Island. The original trees were buried under lime-laden sand, calcified, then exposed by wind action.*

OPPOSITE RIGHT: *The windswept Tongue Point, on Flinders Island, stretches towards Cape Barren Island in the distance — the second largest island in the Furneaux group.*

## The wreck of the Cataraqui

Bass Strait was a graveyard for ships last century and today the waters around both King and Flinders islands are dotted with wrecks. The worst of the disasters occurred on 4 August 1845 when the emigrant ship, *Cataraqui*, struck a reef on the south-western side of King Island during a wild gale.

The barque, bound for Melbourne from Liverpool, was carrying 370 passengers and 46 crew. Within half an hour of hitting the reef she careened over and about 200 passengers were washed overboard. By daybreak, there were only about 30 people still alive on the wreck which was being pounded by heavy seas. Only nine reached the shore alive, and among them was Solomon Brown, an emigrant whose wife and children were drowned, and the first mate, Thomas Guthrie.

News of the disaster reached Melbourne a month later and the subsequent inquiry led to the establishment of lighthouses on King Island and along the Victorian coast. One of those lighthouses, Cape Wickham, on the northern tip of the island, is now among King Island's most photographed sights.

There was a grim finale for both Solomon Brown and Thomas Guthrie. Brown was drowned about three years later in a creek near Port Phillip in Victoria. The water was only half a metre deep. Guthrie, too, was drowned. A year after the wreck of the *Cataraqui*, he was the skipper of a ship which was wrecked near Adelaide. He swam ashore to get help and was the only man drowned.

Ironically, the name, 'Cataraqui', is an Iroquois Indian word from Canada — one translation of this unusual name is 'where rocks meet water'.

The
North-West

# THE NORTH-WEST

*A land in bloom*

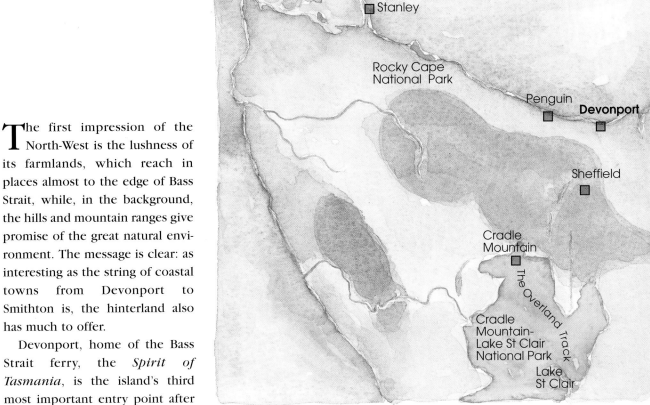

The first impression of the North-West is the lushness of its farmlands, which reach in places almost to the edge of Bass Strait, while, in the background, the hills and mountain ranges give promise of the great natural environment. The message is clear: as interesting as the string of coastal towns from Devonport to Smithton is, the hinterland also has much to offer.

Devonport, home of the Bass Strait ferry, the *Spirit of Tasmania*, is the island's third most important entry point after Hobart and Launceston, and is the closest to Cradle Mountain. The trip inland via the delightful town of Sheffield — famed for its life-size murals depicting local people and events — takes less than 90 minutes and the Mole Creek Caves are also within easy reach.

The Cradle Mountain-Lake St Clair National Park, part of Tasmania's spectacular World Heritage area, contains the Overland Track — a challenge which draws some 5000 bushwalkers each year. The walk, of about 70 kilometres, takes five to six days, and most opt to conclude the experience with a ferry ride down the length of Lake St Clair. The Cradle Mountain Lodge provides good accommodation and a wide range of environmental experiences.

A feature of the North-West Coast, particularly in spring, is its gardens and the region is

LEFT: *Important Aboriginal rock carvings, shell middens and other signs of early habitation can be found near this spectacular beach at Mt Cameron West north of Arthur River.*
PREVIOUS PAGES: *Tulips in bloom at a bulb farm near Wynyard, on the North-West Coast.*

very much the centrepiece of the 'Blooming Tasmania' image. The Emu Valley Rhododendron Gardens in Burnie attract international attention, while perhaps the absolute highlight of spring occurs on the top of Table Cape at Wynyard where a bulb farm produces hectares of tulips and is backed by the local tulip festival.

The coastal scenery is at its best heading west from Wynyard. Boat Harbour has a glorious white-sand beach, and the adjacent Rocky Cape National Park is well worth a visit for its walks and traces of Aboriginal occupation. Stanley, lying in the shadow of the Nut — a 150-metre volcanic plug — is, together with Richmond

and Ross, one of Tasmania's best preserved historic towns. Founded in the 1830s by the Van Diemen's Land Company, it has many historic buildings, some over 150 years old, and was the birthplace of Joseph Lyons, the only Tasmanian to become prime minister. On the outskirts of the town, Highfield, a farming property, was built as the headquarters of the company, and is now maintained by the Parks & Wildlife Service and is open for inspection. Stanley has a nationally recognised arts festival, with the work of many of the state's best artists and craftspeople available in various shops and galleries.

Several forestry reserves inland from Stanley and Smithton are equipped with picnic facilities and give an insight into the state's magnificent rainforests. Just south of Smithton are the Allendale Gardens — two hectares of gardens created on the edge of a patch of rainforest to which they are linked. Allendale closes only in the middle of winter. Less than an hour south-west of Smithton is the Arthur River where a five-hour cruise can be made on the MV *George Robinson*. The boat cruises 14 kilometres upstream into the rainforest and passengers are able to go ashore for a short bushwalk followed by a barbecue. The opportunity to feed a pair of sea eagles is a highlight of the return journey.

RIGHT TOP: *A picturesque striped lighthouse stands on Mersey Bluff, Devonport — the gateway to Cradle Mountain and the North-West Coast.*

RIGHT: *Devonport Cup Day is one of the highlights of the thoroughbred racing year in northern Tasmania.*

FAR RIGHT: *The Bass Strait vehicular ferry, the* Spirit of Tasmania, *makes three return crossings from Melbourne to Devonport each week carrying passengers, their cars, tour coaches and freight vehicles.*

## Tasmanian tiger

The great unanswered question is whether the Tasmanian tiger, or more properly the marsupial wolf, still exists. Certainly it lives on in the state's official brand and marketing image and in the name of the Tasmanian cricket team, but it is more than 60 years since the death of the last animal in captivity and longer still since the last one was shot in the wild (at Mawbanna in the far North-West in 1930). Even so, it's a rare year that there is not a reported sighting — almost always at night and never with time to look for a camera!

The 'tiger' gained its name from the stripes which stretched across its back from behind the neck to the rump, and large specimens measured about two metres from nose to tail. The animal was hunted almost to extinction from the mid-1830s to the turn of the century, with bounties being paid by landowners, then the state government. In 20 years the government paid cash for the scalps of 2184 tigers. Now, in its apparent absence, the mantle of the nation's largest marsupial carnivore passes to the Tasmanian Devil, a star at every wildlife park on the island and some nocturnal bush walks. The Devil is a carrion eater possessed of extremely powerful jaws, and is particularly common on the East Coast. Despite its fearsome snarls it poses no threat to people.

Cradle
Mountain-□□
Lake St Clair
National Park

Walls of
Jerusalem
National Park

RIGHT: *A colourful gnarled snow gum grows beside Lake St Clair at the southern end of the world-famous Overland Track.*

FAR RIGHT: *Lucky bushwalkers on a glorious day gather at Suicide Rock, above Dove Lake, in the Cradle Mountain-Lake St Clair National Park. The walk around Dove Lake is popular with day visitors, but Cradle Mountain is often shrouded in cloud and mist.*

MIDDLE RIGHT: *Two types of currawongs are found in Tasmania — the black and the grey.*

BOTTOM RIGHT: *The Walls of Jerusalem National Park, 90 kilometres south of Devonport and one of the most unusual and spectacular parks in Australia, resembles an amphitheatre with lakes and forests dwarfed by towering escarpments.*

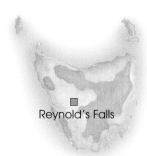

Reynold's Falls

RIGHT: *A frosty Pool of Memories is part of the magic of the Cradle Mountain-Lake St Clair National Park, and is near the famous Overland Track.*

FAR RIGHT: *Snow-capped mountains skirt the beautiful Lake St Clair. Carved out by a glacier during the last Ice Age, it is the deepest natural lake in Australia and is also the source of the Derwent River. A ferry service operating from Cynthia Bay collects bushwalkers from the Overland Track and carries sightseers on lake cruises.*

BELOW RIGHT: *Reynold's Falls, on the Vale River in the North-West, plunges 60 metres from a notch in a 90-metre rock face.*

RIGHT AND BELOW RIGHT: *The North-West Coast has some of the finest farming land in Australia, with dairying and cropping key components.*

OPPOSITE: *Colourful wildflowers grow beside the road on the outskirts of the small North-West Coast town of Penguin, named after the fairy penguin rookeries in the area.*

BELOW: *Sheffield, 30 minutes inland from Devonport, is known as the town of murals as a result of a community project which reflects the region's history and environment.*

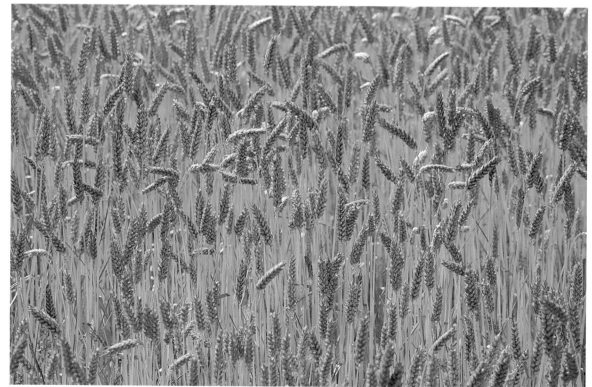

☐ The Nut

ABOVE: *The Stanley Craft Centre, an award-winning venture, helps maintain the town's reputation as an important centre for arts and crafts.*

FAR RIGHT: *A chairlift carries visitors to the flat-topped summit of the Nut at Stanley for sweeping views of the North-West Coast and its hinterland.*

RIGHT: *The ruins of 'Highfield', the original head-quarters of the Van Diemens Land Company, are being restored and are open for inspection.*

# Index

# *Acknowledgements*

*I* consider many of the images in this publication to have come about as a team effort. Quite often friends and even strangers have gone out of their way to help me, and whilst I cannot thank them all individually, some deserve special mention.

Denny Hamill has spent most of his life living and working on the West Coast of Tasmania. Our paths crossed quite by chance as I was preparing to head up the Gordon and Franklin Rivers. Having visited the Gordon as a child, worked there with the piners as a young adult and taken countless tourists there as the skipper of the *J Lee M*, Denny knows this region like few others. He has been instrumental in introducing me to some breathtaking locations, many of which provided the inspiration for this book.

The Grining Family has been operating tourist vessels on Macquarie Harbour and the Gordon River since the turn of the century. They currently own and operate the vessel *Wanderer II*, which makes daily trips into the World Heritage area. From my very first trip up the River, the family and their staff have gone out of their way to help me. Providing me with transport and provisions, they have enabled me to remain on the River for weeks at times, thus providing me with the opportunity of capturing this magnificent wilderness at its best.

Craig Johnson lives and works in Smithton on the North West Coast. He is an avid bushwalker and photographer who has introduced many friends to the exhilarating pleasures of walking in the Cradle Mt region. Due to radical weather changes in the highlands, you must carry additional food and clothing combined with other essentials such as tents, cooking equipment and copious amounts of chocolate. By the time these items are packed there is little room left for heavy cameras, lenses and tripods. Craig has often helped me carry that extra weight, enabling me to spend precious time in remote locations.

I would also like to thank Diane Coon & Ian Brokenshire, Ossie Ellis, Di Coon, Anka Markovac, Jo and Gordon Cuff, Wilderness Air and Trowunna Wildlife Park for their support and hospitality.

Joe Shemesh

*M*y thanks to Delia Nicholls of Tourism Tasmania and to Tony Marshall of the Tasmaniana Library in Hobart for their assistance. I am also grateful to staff of the Parks & Wildlife Service, and to all those tourism operators who ensure that Tasmania's great natural environment is backed by a friendly welcome to visitors.

Mike Bingham